Easter Egg Disaster

A Harry & Emily Adventure

Karen Gray Ruelle

Holiday House / New York

In memory
of Megaphone

Reading level: 2.2

Printed in the United States of America
www.holidayhouse.com
First Edition
1 3 5 7 9 10 8 6 4 2

Library of Congress Cataloging-in-Publication Data
Ruelle, Karen Gray.
Easter egg disaster / Karen Gray Ruelle.—1st ed.
p. cm.
Summary: Harry and Emily, cat siblings, make a mess
when they try to dye and hide Easter eggs.
ISBN 0-8234-1806-5 (hardcover)
ISBN 0-8234-1823-5 (paperback)
[1. Easter eggs—Fiction. 2. Easter—Fiction.
3. Brothers and sisters—Fiction. 4. Cats—Fiction.]
I. Title.
PZ7.R88525 Eaq 2004
[E]—dc21
2003047844

Contents

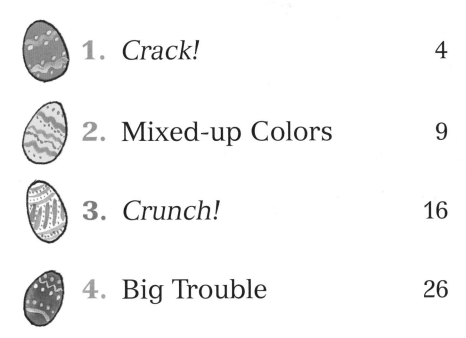

1. *Crack!*   4

2. Mixed-up Colors   9

3. *Crunch!*   16

4. Big Trouble   26

1.

Crack!

"That is not how you make
  an Easter egg," said Emily.
Her big brother, Harry,
  put down his egg.
"You are doing it wrong,"
  said Emily.

4

She picked up an egg.

She picked out a pink crayon.

She drew on the egg.

CRACK!

The egg broke.

"I drew too hard," said Emily.

She picked up another egg.

She picked out a green crayon.

CRACK!

"If you are so smart," said Emily,

"why don't you show me!"

"First, you get the egg
    out of the shell," said Harry.
    He poked two holes
    in an eggshell.
    He blew through one hole.
    Raw egg dripped
    out of the other hole.

"Yuck!" said Emily.

"Let me try."

Harry poked holes
in another shell.
Emily blew hard.
Nothing happened.
She blew harder.
Nothing happened.
She squeezed the egg hard.
The shell broke.
"I got the egg out," said Emily.

"But we cannot decorate
  a broken shell," said Harry.
"There must be a better way
  to make Easter eggs," said Emily.
"We can hard-boil the eggs,"
  said Harry.
"Then we can decorate them."
"Yum," said Emily.
"I like hard-boiled eggs."

2.
Mixed-up Colors

"We have six hard-boiled eggs

to decorate," said Harry.

He picked out a white crayon.

He drew a bunny on an egg.

He used green

and red crayons for flowers.

Then he dipped the bottom
of the egg in green dye.
He dipped the rest of
the egg in blue dye.
The dye did not stick
to the crayon drawing.
But it colored the rest of the shell.
Harry's egg had a white bunny
and red and green tulips.
It had green grass
and a blue sky.

Emily said, "Let me do one."
She drew a pink chick
and a purple flower.
"I want a yellow sky," she said.
She dipped the egg in yellow dye.
"That looks funny," she said.
"I will make it blue instead."

She dipped the yellow egg
in blue dye.
"It turned green!" she said.
"That is what happens when you
  mix colors together," said Harry.
"Yellow and blue make green."
"What a great trick!" said Emily.
"What other colors can you make?"
"Let's find out," said Harry.

They mixed red and blue.

It made purple.

They mixed red and yellow.

It made orange.

They mixed red and yellow
and blue.

"That looks like mud," said Emily.

In the end, all six eggs had pretty crayon drawings.

But all six eggs were mud-brown.

"These eggs are ugly," said Emily. "I think we should hide them."

"What a great idea!" said Harry. "We can make an Easter egg hunt for Mom and Dad. We can use chocolate eggs, too."

"Ooh, I love chocolate eggs," said Emily.

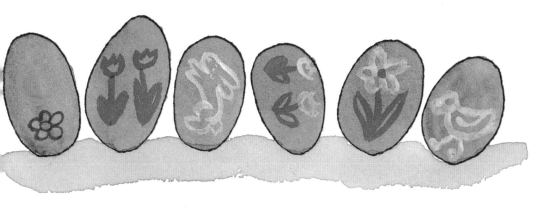

3.
Crunch!

It was the day before Easter.
"Let's hide the eggs now,"
said Emily,
"before the Easter Bunny comes."
They looked for good spots.
They found a good spot
for a dyed egg
under a chair cushion.
They found two good spots
in a pair of boots.
There were good hiding spots
for chocolate eggs, too.

They put some in a glove.

They put some in a hat.

The best hiding spots were

in the kitchen.

"Let's put chocolate eggs

in this empty pan," said Emily.

They also put chocolate eggs

in the oven.

"Let's put some dyed eggs in the egg

tray in the fridge," said Harry.

"I can't wait for Easter!" said Emily.

Later that day,
Harry and Emily's parents began
to get ready for Easter.
"Daffodils would look pretty
on the table," said their mother.
"I will get some from the garden,"
said their father.
"Here are your gardening gloves
and hat," said their mother.
She put them down on the radiator.

"It is muddy outside," she said.

"You will need your boots."

Their father put on his boots.

CRUNCH! CRUNCH!

"What was that?" he asked.

He sat down on the chair

to remove his boots.

CRUNCH!

There was crushed egg everywhere.

"Who put these eggs here?"

he asked.

He was angry.

He cleaned up the mess.

Then he picked up his hat

and gardening gloves.

"I will go and

pick those flowers now," he said.

He put on his gloves.

He put on his hat.

"Who put chocolate in my hat
and my gloves?"

he said in a very angry voice.

Harry and Emily's mother started
to make dinner.

She chopped onions and peppers.
She put them in a pan with oil.
Then she turned on the oven.
Soon there was a burning smell.
She opened the oven door.
There was chocolate burning
in the oven.
"Who put chocolate in here?"
    she asked.

The onions and peppers
were getting hot.
She stirred them.
The spoon turned brown.
"How did chocolate get in the pan?

Now dinner is ruined.

The oven is a mess," she said.

"I'll have to make

something else for dinner.

How about an omelette?"

She opened the refrigerator.

"What happened to all the eggs?"

she asked.

There were no uncooked eggs.

They were all hard-boiled

and decorated for Easter.

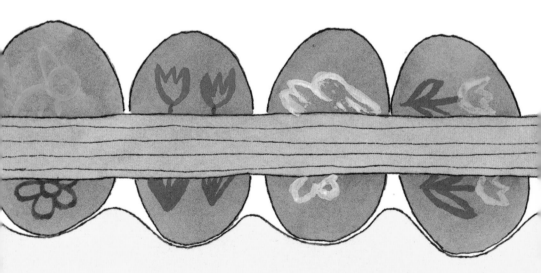

4.
Big Trouble

Harry and Emily were in trouble.

"We didn't mean to make a mess,"
said Harry.

"We were trying to make you
an Easter egg hunt," said Emily.

"Instead of an Easter egg hunt,
you made an Easter egg disaster,"
said their mother.

"Clean up this mess,"
said their father.

When they went to bed that night,
Harry and Emily were worried.

"What if Mom and Dad are still
mad in the morning?" said Harry.
"What if they don't let
the Easter Bunny come?"
said Emily.
Harry could not sleep
all night.
Emily had bad dreams
about no Easter candy.

The next morning,

Harry and Emily came

down to breakfast.

There were no Easter baskets

in their rooms.

The Easter Bunny had not come.

Would they even have Easter at all?

Were their parents still angry?

"Good morning," said their mother.

"We are sorry about the mess
we made," said Harry.

"We made you an Easter card,"
said Emily.

She gave their parents the Easter card.

"It is also an apology card," she said.

"Apology accepted," said their father.